P9-BBU-012

A Treasury of Bible Stories

Retold by
Pamela Broughton

🐣 *A Golden® Book* • NEW YORK

Golden Books Publishing Company, Inc.
New York, New York 10106

Library of Congress Catalog Number: 99-62366
ISBN: 0-307-10382-X

© 1999 Golden Books Publishing Company, Inc.

Table of Contents

The Creation

Genesis 1, 2:1-3

In the beginning, God created the heavens and the earth.

At first, darkness was everywhere.

God said, "Let there be light." At once there was bright light. God moved the light apart from the darkness. He called the light day and the darkness night.

God saw that the light was good. There was evening and morning, the first day.

9

Then God made the sky, to divide the waters. There were waters above the sky, and waters below.

God saw that the sky was good. There was evening and morning, the second day.

11

12

God said, "Let all the waters under the sky be gathered into one place. Let the dry land appear."

It was so, and God called the dry land earth. The waters He called seas.

God saw that the earth and the seas were good.

God made plants and grasses to cover the land.
He made trees, with fruit hanging from the branches.
He made each growing thing to have seeds, that
more growing things like it might come to be.

God looked at what He had made, and He saw that it was good. And there was evening and morning, the third day.

And God said, "Let there be different lights in the sky, to serve as signs, to mark the days and the seasons and the years."

God made the sun to light the earth by day.

He made the moon to light the earth by night. He made the stars as well.

God saw that it was good. And there was evening and morning, the fourth day.

Then God said, "Let the seas be filled with living creatures." And He created great whales and little fishes and every creature that lives in the sea.

And God said, "Let birds fly through the sky." He created all the birds of the air, every creature that has wings. And they flew, and the sky was full of them.

God saw that all He had made was good. He blessed the living creatures that swim and fly. There was evening and morning, the fifth day.

Then God said, "Let there be living creatures to walk upon the earth."

God created cattle and creeping things and all the beasts that live on land. And God saw that it was good.

Then God created man and woman.

God said, "Let man and woman rule over the fishes of the sea, the birds of the sky, over all the earth and the beasts that live on it."

God blessed man and woman. He said, "Fill the earth with your children. Rule over the creatures of the sea, the birds of the air, and the beasts of the earth. See the grasses and plants and trees with fruit—these shall be for food for you and every living thing." And it was so.

God saw that everything He had made was very good. And there was evening and morning, the sixth day.

Then God rested from the work that He had done. And He blessed the seventh day, and made it a holy day of rest.

NOAH'S ARK

Genesis 6:5-9:17

The people of the world had become very wicked.

In all the world, God found only one good person, a man named Noah.

God called to Noah and said, "I will bring a flood upon the earth. Everything on the earth will die."

God told Noah to build an ark of wood. He told him to cover it with tar, inside and out.

"In the ark, you and your family will be safe from the flood. Bring along two of each kind of animal, male and female. And bring enough food to feed all the creatures for many days."

Noah told his family all that God had said.

The next day, Noah and his three sons began to build the ark.

Their wives went to gather food for their time in the
ark.

After much hard work, the ark was ready. Then God spoke to Noah again.

God said, "Seven days from now, I will bring a great rain upon the earth. It will rain for forty days and forty nights."

And God said, "I will send you male and female of each kind of bird and animal, and of every kind of creeping thing.

"Bring the animals into the ark with you, to keep them alive."

41

Noah went into the ark after all the animals were safe inside. And his wife and his sons and his sons' wives all went into the ark, too.

Then God shut the door of the ark and sealed it. The rain began.

For forty days and forty nights, the rain did not stop.
The water rose higher and higher.
Noah's ark floated on the waves.

The mountains were covered with water.
Everything that God had made died on the face of
the earth.

Only Noah and those in the ark with him were left alive.

After forty days and forty nights, just as God had said, the rain stopped. Soon the water started to go down. The ark came to rest atop a great mountain.

Noah opened the window of the ark. He sent out a dove to see if the earth was dry. But the dove could not find a dry place to land, and she returned to the ark.

Seven days later, Noah sent out the dove again. She came back with an olive leaf in her beak. Noah knew that the water still covered all but the highest treetops.

After seven more days, Noah sent out the dove again. This time the dove did not come back. She had found a dry place to make her nest. The earth was dry again.

God told Noah to come out of the ark. So Noah, his family, and all the animals stepped out onto dry land.

Noah built an altar to worship God.

God was pleased, and He made a promise to Noah. "I will never again send a flood to kill all the living things on earth," He said. "The rainbow is a sign of this promise. When you see the rainbow in the sky, you will know that I remember my promise for all time."

Joseph and the Coat of Many Colors

Genesis 37:3-36, 39:1-45:15

Jacob was an old man who had twelve sons. He
lived with them in the land called Canaan.

Jacob loved one son, Joseph, best of all. He gave
Joseph a coat of many colors, to show his love.

That made Joseph's brothers jealous.

A short time later, Joseph had two dreams. In the first dream, he and his brothers were tying bundles of grain in a field. Joseph's bundle rose up, and his brothers' bundles bowed down before it.

In the second dream, the sun, the moon, and eleven
stars bowed down before Joseph.

Joseph told his brothers and his father about the
dreams. His father said, "Shall I and your mother and
brothers bow down before you?"

Then Joseph's brothers grew more jealous.

One day, when the brothers were caring for their
sheep in the fields, Jacob sent Joseph to bring back
news of them.

When the brothers saw Joseph coming, they decided
to kill him.

But the oldest brother, Reuben, said, "Let's throw Joseph into a pit, but let's not kill him," for Reuben meant to rescue Joseph.

When Joseph reached the place, his brothers took his many-colored coat. They threw Joseph into a deep hole.

Soon a camel caravan passed on its way to Egypt.
Reuben was away. His brother Judah suggested that
they sell Joseph to the caravan traders, to be a slave.
All the brothers agreed.

After they had sold Joseph, the brothers took his coat and dipped it in the blood of an animal. Then they took the coat to their father.

When Jacob saw the coat, he thought Joseph had been killed by a wild beast. He wept for his lost son, and refused to be comforted.

But God was with Joseph.

In Egypt, he was sold to Potiphar, the captain of the king's guard. Potiphar liked Joseph, and put him in charge of his household.

Potiphar's wife hated Joseph, and she told lies about him to her husband. So at last, Potiphar had Joseph thrown into prison.

The chief jailer liked Joseph. He put Joseph in charge of all the other prisoners.

One day, the king grew angry with his cupbearer and his baker. He had them thrown into the prison.

A night came when they each had a dream. The next morning, they told their dreams to Joseph. Joseph knew that God would help him understand the dreams. He was able to tell them what their dreams meant: The baker was to be killed, but the cupbearer would be released to serve the king again.

Joseph said to the cupbearer, "Remember me when it goes well with you, for I have done nothing wrong."

In three days, the baker was hanged and the cupbearer stood before the king again, just as Joseph had said.

But the cupbearer forgot about Joseph.

Two years later, the king had a dream, and no one could tell him what it meant. Then the cupbearer remembered Joseph, who was still in prison. Joseph was brought before the king.

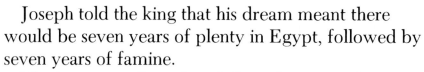

Joseph told the king that his dream meant there would be seven years of plenty in Egypt, followed by seven years of famine.

The king was pleased with Joseph. He put him in charge of the whole kingdom, to build storehouses for the extra food that would grow during the years of plenty.

Just as Joseph had said, the crops grew well for
seven years. Joseph stored the extra grain.

After seven years, there was famine everywhere.
Only in Egypt was there plenty to eat, because of the
grain Joseph had stored.

There was no food in Canaan, where Jacob and his sons lived. So Jacob sent his sons to Egypt to buy food. He did not send Benjamin with them. Benjamin was his youngest son, and Jacob was afraid something might happen to him.

When Jacob's sons came to Egypt, they went to Joseph and bowed before him, just as Joseph's dream had foretold.

Joseph recognized his brothers, but they did not recognize him.

Joseph questioned them about their homeland and their family. Then Joseph said, "You are spies!"

"No," the brothers replied. "We came to buy food."

"If you are honest men," Joseph said, "one of you will remain here while the rest bring food to your family. Then come back with your youngest brother."

One brother remained in Egypt, while the others returned home. When the food was all eaten, Jacob told his sons to return to Egypt and buy more grain. He told them to take Benjamin back with them. "Return to the great ruler in Egypt. And God grant that he may release your brother and send you all safely home."

So they took presents for Joseph, and returned to Egypt.

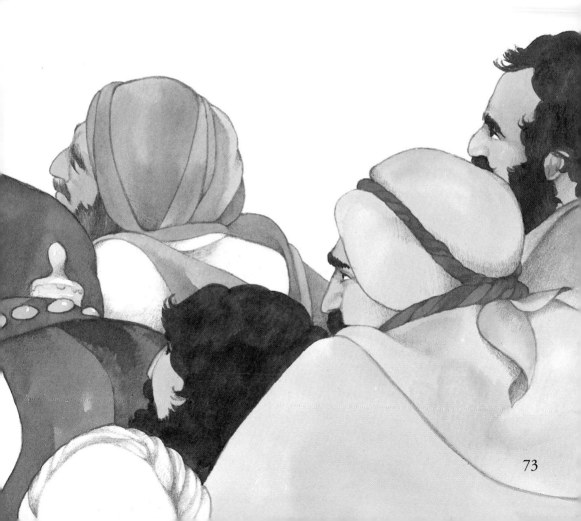

When Joseph saw his brothers, he ordered his servants to bring them to his house. The brothers were surprised when Joseph sat down with them to eat a meal.

Joseph gave them grain. Then he told his servants to hide a silver cup in Benjamin's sack. The brothers left.

Joseph sent his servants after them, to accuse them of stealing the cup. Joseph wanted to make his brothers come back, so he could tell them who he was. The brothers were brought back to Joseph's house.

Joseph told them then that he was their brother. He told them to return to Canaan and bring all Jacob's family back with them to Egypt, to live in honor and plenty.

"Now you see," he said, "you did not send me here. God sent me, to save you and all my people from hunger."

David and Goliath

I Samuel 17:1-51

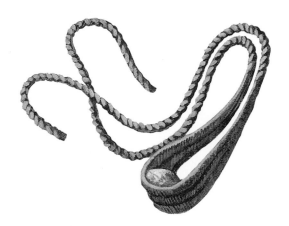

There was a war in the land of Israel. The Philistine armies had come to fight, and they were ready and waiting in their mountaintop camp.

King Saul and the men of Israel were ready, too.
They waited atop another mountain, across the valley.

A champion came out of the Philistine camp. He was a giant named Goliath of Gath. He cried to the men of Israel, "Choose a champion for yourselves. If he is able to kill me, then the Philistines will be your servants. But if I kill him, then you shall be our servants. Give me a man to fight!"

When Saul and the men of Israel heard these words, they were greatly afraid. They did not have a man who could defeat the giant.

Now there was a boy named David, and he was the youngest of eight sons. While three of his older brothers served in the army, David took care of his father's sheep in Bethlehem.

One day David's father sent for him. He told David
to take some food to his brothers and their captain,
and to bring back news of the war.

David awoke early the next morning. He took the food and set out for King Saul's camp.

When he arrived, David left the food with the
supply keeper. Then he went to find his brothers.

As David talked with his brothers, Goliath came out again to challenge the army of Israel.

When the men of Israel saw Goliath, they were frightened and ran away.

Some men said to David, "Do you see this giant?
King Saul will give riches and his own daughter in
marriage to the man who can kill him."

And David said, "Who is this Philistine to threaten the army of the living God?"

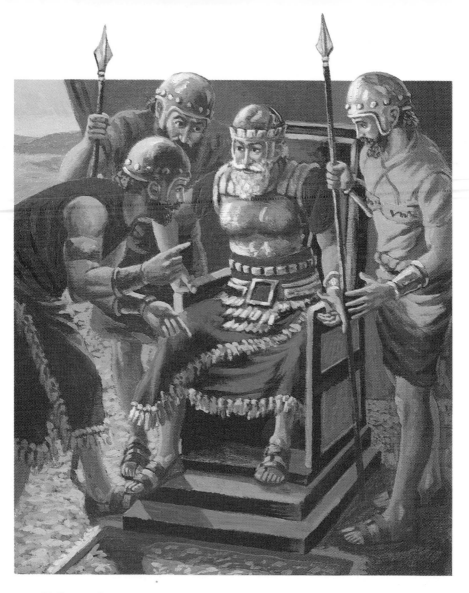

When the people heard David's words, they ran to tell them to King Saul. Then Saul sent for David.

David said, "Let no one fear Goliath. I will go and fight this man."

But Saul said, "You cannot fight him. You are just a boy, and he is a trained soldier."

David said to King Saul, "I kept my father's sheep. A lion came, and it took a lamb out of the flock. And I went out after the lamb and took it from the lion's mouth. I killed the lion. This giant shall be like that lion. The Lord who delivered me from the lion will deliver me from this Philistine."

And Saul said to David, "Go, and the Lord be with you."

93

King Saul gave David his own armor to wear in the battle. David tried it on. Then he said, "I cannot wear this armor. I am not used to it."

And he took off Saul's armor.

David took up his staff. He picked five smooth stones out of a brook and put them in his shepherd's bag. He took his sling and went out to meet Goliath.

When the Philistine saw David with his staff, he said, "Am I a dog that you come to me with sticks?"

David answered, "You come to me with a sword and a shield. But I come to you in the name of the Lord, the God of the army of Israel. This day the Lord will deliver you into my hand, that all the earth may know there is a God in Israel."

David put his hand in his bag and took out a stone. He put the stone in his sling and took careful aim. Then he swung the sling and let go. The stone struck the Philistine's forehead, and Goliath fell to the ground.

David ran and took Goliath's sword and cut off the giant's head.

When the Philistines saw that their champion was dead, they grew afraid and ran away. The men of Israel ran after them and drove them off.

So David defeated the Philistines with a sling and a stone, and the help of the living God.

JESUS
at the Temple

Luke 2:22-52

After Jesus was born, Mary and Joseph took the baby to Jerusalem, to present him to the Lord at the great Temple there.

There was a man in Jerusalem named Simeon. God had told Simeon that he would see God's special Son before he died.

When Mary and Joseph brought Jesus to the Temple, Simeon was there.

Simeon took Jesus into his arms. He knew that Jesus was God's Son.

He said, "Now, Lord, I will die in peace. You have sent one who will save the lost people of our land."

Then Simeon blessed Mary and Joseph. He gave
Jesus back to them.

An old widow named Anna was also in the Temple.
Anna came up to Mary and Joseph, and thanked God.

She told everyone that God's Son had come.

When they had done everything according to the law of God, Mary and Joseph took Jesus and returned to Nazareth, their home in Galilee.

The child grew and became strong. And his
wisdom and understanding grew, too.   111

When Jesus was twelve years old, his parents again took him to Jerusalem. This time they went to celebrate the Feast of Passover at the Temple.

After celebrating for seven days, Mary and Joseph
set out for home. But Jesus stayed behind.

Jesus's parents did not know this. They thought he was traveling home with some others who were also returning to Nazareth.

But after they had gone a day's journey, they began to look for him.

They could not find him there. So they went all the
way back to Jerusalem to look for him.

After three days of searching, they finally found
him in the Temple. Jesus was sitting with the teachers,
listening to them and asking them questions.

All who heard him were amazed at his understanding and wisdom.

When his parents found him, Mary said, "Son, why
have you treated us so? We have been trying to find
you, and we've been terribly worried."   119

"Why were you looking for me?" Jesus asked. "Did you not know I would stay here at the Temple, doing 120 my Father's business?"

His parents did not understand his words.

But Jesus returned to Nazareth with them, and was an obedient son.

Mary lovingly kept all these things in her heart.

Jesus grew tall and wise, and was loved by God
and man.

124

The Life of Jesus

Jesus

Adapted from the Gospels
According to Matthew and John

A long time ago, a man named John heard good news from God. God's Son was coming to live on earth.

John went through the country, telling people the news. The people believed the news. They followed John to the River Jordan. There John baptized them in the water.   127

One day Jesus came to be baptized. Jesus was John's cousin.

When John saw Jesus, he said, "This is the Son of God."

After He was baptized, Jesus went into the desert to pray. There He met the devil.

Jesus had no food in the desert. He went forty days without eating. The devil tempted Him, saying, "If You are the Son of God, change these stones to bread."

But Jesus said, "Man does not live by bread alone."

The devil showed Jesus all the kingdoms of the world. He said, "Serve me, and You will rule the world."

But Jesus said, "You shall worship the Lord your God and serve Him only."

The devil took Jesus to the top of the Temple at Jerusalem. "Jump off," he said. "God will not allow His Son to be hurt." But Jesus would not.

He told the devil, "God says, 'Do not test Me.'"
The devil saw that he could not make Jesus serve him. So the devil sneaked away until a better time. And angels came and helped Jesus.

Then Jesus returned home and began to teach the
Word of God. News about Him spread through the
country.

Some men who heard the news decided to follow Jesus. They were called disciples. Their names were John, James, Andrew, Peter, Philip, Nathanael, Thomas, Matthew, Simon, Thaddeus, and James, the son of Alphaeus.

Another man decided to follow Jesus, too. His name was Judas.

The disciples learned about God from Jesus, and they helped Jesus teach others.

Now there were people called Pharisees who did
not like the things Jesus said. They wanted to stop Him
from teaching. But they could not stop His followers
from spreading news of the wonderful things Jesus did.

One day, Jesus went to a wedding in a small town called Cana. During the celebration, the wine ran out.

Jesus told the servants to fill six stone jars with water. Then He told them to pour some out. The water had turned to wine, and there was enough for all the guests.

After this, Jesus and His disciples were at the pool of Siloam. There lived a man who had been born blind.

Jesus spat on the ground to make clay. He put the clay on the man's eyes and told him to wash in the pool. The man did what Jesus said. When he came back, he could see.

The man was brought before the Pharisees. They said to him, "This Jesus only pretends to be from God. He is nothing more than a magician who does wicked tricks."

But the man said, "I only know that I was blind, and now I see. If Jesus were not from God, He could not make me see."

But the Pharisees wanted to punish Jesus.

Jesus heard that His friend Lazarus was very sick. After two days, Jesus said, "Lazarus is dead now. But I will wake him."

The disciples were afraid. They knew the Pharisees would punish them if they heard any more about Jesus' "tricks."

But Jesus was not afraid. When He reached His
friend's house, Lazarus's sister ran out to meet Him.

"Lord," she said, "if You had been here, my brother
would not have died. Even now, I know that God will
grant whatever You ask."

Jesus said, "Your brother shall rise again."

They went to Lazarus's grave. They removed the stone that covered the grave, and Jesus prayed to God. Then Jesus said, "Lazarus, come forth!"

Lazarus came out of the grave. He was alive!

Then many people believed that Jesus was from God. But the devil saw that a better time had come and that his evil could succeed. He told Judas to go to the Pharisees. Now Judas was not a good man, as the other disciples were. So he listened to the devil. He told the Pharisees that he would help them arrest Jesus.

143

Jesus and His disciples were in the garden of Gethsemane. The Pharisees sent Judas there with soldiers to take Jesus away.

Jesus was beaten, and a crown of thorns was placed on His head. Then He was nailed to a cross.

After Jesus had hung on the cross for nine hours, the sky grew dark. Jesus said, "It is finished," and He died.

His followers took His body away for burial.

Two days later, some of Jesus' friends went to pray by Jesus' tomb. They were surprised by what they found—the stone that covered the tomb had been removed, and the tomb was empty.

An angel sat before the tomb. He said, "Do not be afraid. I know that you are looking for Jesus, but He is not here. He has risen. You will see Him and speak with Him again."

The disciples were overjoyed when they met Jesus, the risen Lord. Jesus taught the disciples more about God's love.

"Rejoice!" He said. "For I am with you always, even to the end of the world."

The Miracle of the Loaves and Fishes

Mark 6:30-46, *John* 6:1-15

One time, Jesus sent out his disciples to teach people
and heal people far and wide.

When the disciples returned, they wanted to tell
Jesus what they had done and taught while they were
away.

But the town was crowded and noisy, and the disciples had not had time to eat.

Jesus said, "Let us go to a quiet place and rest awhile."

So they rowed across the Sea of Galilee to a quiet place.

The people saw Jesus leaving. They saw where he was going, and took a shorter way to the quiet place.

When Jesus reached the other shore, people were already gathered there.

The people seemed like lost sheep. Jesus knew that they needed him to be their shepherd. So he healed those who were sick, and he comforted those who were unhappy.

Then Jesus went up on a mountain with his disciples.

He looked down and saw that there were many,
many people in the crowd.

It grew late. Jesus said, "Give them something to eat."

The disciple Philip said, "Two hundred silver coins would not buy enough food for all of them."

The disciples thought Jesus would send them to buy food in the nearby villages.

But Jesus said, "How much food is there? Go and see."

The disciple Andrew answered, "There is a boy with five loaves of barley bread and two small fishes. But how can we feed so many people with so little food?"

Jesus said, "Make the people sit down."
The disciples told the people to sit down in the green grass. There were about five thousand men in the crowd, and many women and children.

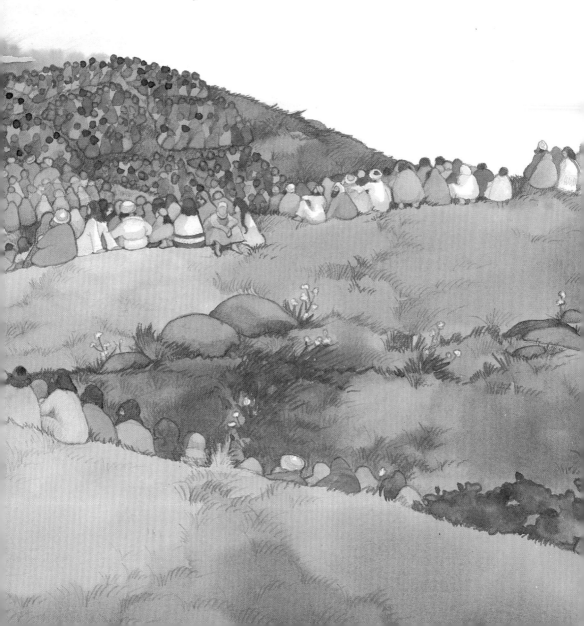

Jesus took the five loaves and two fishes. He looked up to heaven. Then he blessed the loaves and broke them. He handed the pieces to his disciples to give to the people.

The fishes, too, were broken and given to the people.

And though it was only a little, and the crowd was huge, there was plenty for everyone after Jesus blessed the food.

When the people had eaten their fill, Jesus told his disciples to gather up the leftover pieces of bread and fish.

They filled twelve big baskets with the pieces that were left after everyone had eaten.

The people wondered at the miracle Jesus had done,
feeding so many people with so little food.

169

Jesus sent the people away.

Then he told his disciples to row back across the sea.

Jesus said he would come to them later. And he went alone up the mountain to pray.

The Prodigal Son

Luke 15:1-3, 11-32

When Jesus taught, all kinds of people gathered
to hear him. Sometimes Jesus ate with the people who
gathered.

Some people said, "Jesus does not care who eats
with him. He even lets bad people eat at his table."

Jesus heard what they said. This is a story he told to
answer them.

There was a rich man who had two sons. He planned to give half his fortune to each son.

One day the younger son said, "Father, give me now my half of your fortune."

So the man divided all he had between his sons.

The younger son gathered his share together and went away to a far country.

There he wasted all he had. Soon everything was
spent.

Then a bad time came to that country, and no one had enough to eat.

The young son began to grow hungry.

So he went out to find work. A man hired him to feed pigs.

No one showed any kindness to the son. He grew so hungry that he would have gladly eaten what the pigs ate.

One day he thought, "Back home, even my father's pig-keeper has more than enough to eat. Yet here I am, dying of hunger."

He said, "I will leave here and go to my father. I will
say, 'Father, I have done wrong. I no longer deserve to
be your son. But let me work for you.'"
And he rose up and went to his father.

When he was still a long way off, his father saw him.

He kissed his son, and hugged him.

The son said, "Father, I have done wrong. I no longer deserve to be your son."

But the father said to his servants, "Bring the best robe, and put it on him. Put a ring on his finger and shoes on his feet."

He said, "Prepare a great feast, and let us eat and be merry. For my son was lost and now is found again." And they began to be merry.

Now the older son was in the fields. And when he
came home, he heard the sounds of music and dancing.
He called one of the servants and asked, "What does
this music and dancing mean?"

The servant answered, "Your brother has come home
safe and sound, so your father has made a feast to
celebrate."

193

The older son was angry and would not join the
feast. So his father left the table and begged him to
194   come.

But the brother said, "I have worked for you all these years. I have never disobeyed you. Yet you never made even a small feast for me and my friends.

"But as soon as this bad, wasteful son comes home, you hold a great feast for him."

And the father said to him, "Son, you are always
with me. All that I have is yours. But it was right for us
to make merry now.

"For your brother was in trouble and now is safe. He
was lost and now is found."